There Is No Time Management
Utilize Time, don't Manage

OrangeBooks Publication

1st Floor, Rajhans Arcade, Mall Road, Kohka, Bhilai, Chhattisgarh 490020

Website: **www.orangebooks.in**

© Copyright, 2024, Author

All rights reserved. No part of this book may be reproduced, stored in a retrieval system, or transmitted, in any form by any means, electronic, mechanical, magnetic, optical, chemical, manual, photocopying, recording or otherwise, without the prior written consent of its writer.

First Edition, 2024

THERE IS NO TIME MANAGEMENT

UTILIZE TIME, DON'T MANAGE

SRIDHAR YERRAMILLI

OrangeBooks Publication
www.orangebooks.in

Dedicated to...

This book is dedicated to my little princess Srimythri Yerramilli who left us all in teaching us a wonderful lesson that "A limited amount of time is available, which is different for every individual, but reduces equally for all." Her time is over, and she merged with the divine and the rest of us are left with her memories.

Gratitude

I am thankful to 17074 Days of My Life, My Mother, my spouse, brothers & Sisters, my Gurus, my colleagues my Surroundings, all knowledge sources and especially my Critics for inspiring me to rejuvenate and pen down this concept, "There is no Time Management".

I express my gratitude to my Life Coach, the famous, Laudable author and executive Coach Robin Sharma for technology driven coaching and mentoring via online sessions and his valuable publications which always inspired me to pen down few books. I offer my gratitude to Sh. Mahesh Nair, Sh. Sudhanshu Goswami, Sh. G. Sreerammurthy, Sh. Bangarayya, and Sh. Y Somayajulu for reviewing this book and adding up their valuable reviews and comments. I also express my heartfelt gratitude to my best half Smt. Sridivya for reviewing the book multiple times and getting it enhanced till published.

Awareness Campaign on Japanese Encephalitis

I, Srimythri Yerramilli, on behalf of Mythri Charitable Trust, and on behalf of founders, my beloved parents wish to convey an important message. Recently, I was attacked by a very deadly virus known as Japanese Encephalitis, which attacks brain.

Unfortunately, this is very fatal and has no cure, but **fortunately** it has a vaccine. We have never heard of this virus, right. This virus attacks 3 children in one million and unfortunately, I was one of them.

Neither my parents knew there is any kind of such virus and a vaccine to prevent the same nor any doctor/ hospital guided us. My parents are missing me a lot and I am also missing them though I can't express. My parents and I don't even want this to happen to any other child. So, we are writing this to you. This infection has put me to an end in only one hour. It doesn't give any time and rapidly deteriorates the brain's function.

It gives early symptoms such as light fever, headache and body pains which are very common symptoms. No such symptoms are taken so seriously by any parent or even doctors. Doctors just administer Paracetamol suspension or any other antibiotic. So, when was it identified?

I was playing till 9:00 PM and got a very high-grade fever (107^0 F) at night 9:30 followed by 3 episodes of seizures in 5 minutes. I was rushed to hospital by 10:00 PM and by 10:30, I went to Coma stage and unfortunately, I could not return home.

I am not narrating this instance to frighten you. My intention is only to make you aware of this deadly disease which has no cure but has a vaccine. I want you to do the following to ensure no other kids and their parents face such instances.

1. Check your child's vaccine chart and check if the vaccine has been given to your child or not. The vaccine is pertaining to **Japanese Encephalitis**.
2. Check with your pediatrician regarding the same and upon your doctor's advice get your child vaccinated followed by a booster dose.
3. Check with your doctor if there are any optional vaccines & get them administered.
4. Also, don't miss any other vaccine in the chart as prevention is better than cure.

Important:

- This Vaccine might have been included in the immunization chart now, so please check the immunization chart of children of 3 years or more on priority basis, born prior to 2018.
- This message is only to create awareness about the virus. Mythri Charitable Trust is neither responsible for administering the vaccine nor the side effects post administration if any. Get this vaccination only upon consultation with your Pediatrician.
- The symptoms of the disease mentioned are only as per our experience and these may change from case to case.

- Mythri Charitable trust or any of its members by any means are neither proposing this vaccination drive nor are they involved with any organization for executing this vaccination drive.
- This message is delivered only in public interest for creating awareness to fellow beings.
  - For More information visit
  - https://mythri-trust.in/our-programs.

Sridivya Yerramilli & Sridhar Yerramilli
On behalf of Srimythri Yerramilli
Founder Directors
For Mythri Charitable Trust

Table Of Contents

1. Introduction _____ 1
2. Definition of Time Management _____ 5
3. Expert Views _____ 7
4. "Expertise in Time Utilization" _____ 14
5. "Role Identification" _____ 18
   Never miss the link anymore _____ 25
6. Planning _____ 27
7. Practice the Roles & Time Slots _____ 40
8. Identify your Time Stealers _____ 49
9. Keeping ourselves Motivated _____ 54
10. Instill the Mechanism for 24X7X365 X (lifetime) _ 57
11. Ethical Time Utilization _____ 59
12. Self -introspection_____ 62
13. Summarizing the formulae _____ 65
14. Final Words_____ 68
    Self-Introspection _____ 72
15. Claim your Coaching Session _____ 73
16. An important return Gift to you, me & World ___ 75

Introduction

Hello readers, thanks for selecting this book "There is no Time Management". The aim of this book is not to demean the existing concept of Time Management. I take the onus of each, and every word used in this knowledge hub & affirm that these are my views. Almost in every nuke and corner of the world, today at this point of time, when I have started to put my thoughts in words, TIME MANAGEMENT trainings may be proceeding in one or the other forms. May be a teacher instructing his/her student, a professor explaining to his research scholar, a parent taking a long class for the benefit of his or her child.

That's fine, but my point is how we can manage something which we don't have. If I ask you to manage the funds which I have in my bank account without giving you my credentials, is it possible? A stupid question Sridhar, that's what you will say. Am I right? Similarly, time is slipping every moment. Almost 10 minutes have passed since I started penning down my thoughts. Right! Then how can someone Manage time?

Let me quote an example which I have used many times in my workshops. Assume that I have taken a one-liter water bottle, filled it with water, dropped a beautiful golden or parrot fish, and pierced a hole down below the bottle. Now what's happening? Yes, you are right, the water level in the bottle is reducing drop by drop. Now presume that the water is time, and the beautiful fish inside is you. How long are you going to survive? Till the time the water level is sufficient for you to live. Am I right? Hopefully yes. Now can we manage the water? Yes, of course, we can try to block the hole and not let the water pass by. But how long and is it a satisfactory solution? I leave this for your thoughts.

But my conclusion is there is no TIME Management. We can only utilize time.

Now some one may question, have a discussion, is management & utilization not the same? People often question me, is proper utilization of time not time management? I simply deny, and you will also do the same by the end of this page.

Let us deal with this question in a separate way. Take out the true meaning of both the words from google or any dictionary and write it down in the space provided below.

MANAGEMENT: _____

_____

_____

_____

_____

_____

UTILIZATION: _____

_____

_____

_____

_____

_____

Hopefully, after the above exercise, you might have started accepting my thoughts that there is only TIME UTILIZATION and there is NO TIME MANAGEMENT.

In short, whatever may be the jargon, the outcome is using time effectively, and then why does this whole page keep on speaking about the difference? That's what one of my critics asked.

My Simple answer is "Words Matter"; they have the power to change everything. If we deliberately use them in wrong ways, we are going to be affected. Since ages we are under false impression of managing something, which we never own. Isn't it? Let us start uttering the words TIME UTILISATION and use time in an effective way. You will see a difference.

Definition of Time Management

Every organization says to their Managerial employees, "WE NEED LEADERS, TRY TO BECOME GOOD LEADERS". But the designation of those employees is MANAGER, you yourself keep calling them "MANAGERS" but want them to be leaders, that's not possible and not reasonable.

How come a Mango become an Orange. I know that the example of Mango and Orange in this scenario is hopeless, because, even if you call the Mango an Orange even for an infinite time, it is not going to change into an Orange. Right?

Replace the Mango and Orange with the words Useful & Useless. If you call any person useless who is useful, will he not become a useless person? Understand, **Words Matter**. If I had direct access to my employer, I would have asked him to change the jargon. Make everyone a leader. Call them leader-1 leader-2 etc. but not Heads, Managers & Supervisors.

Perhaps, I am moving out of the context. Let me come back and instill my thoughts, for sure to make you and of course myself a much better person than who we are.

There is No Time Management, we cannot manage time.

Only Time Utilization, we can only utilize time effectively.

With this we end the debate on the long-standing concept of "TIME MANAGEMENT". Let us now humbly ask TIME MANAGEMENT to step back and handover the charge to TIME UTILIZATION from this moment onwards.

Moving forward, let us learn TIME UTILIZATION and move to a new concept of Ethical Time Utilization in the coming chapters.

But before that, let us see how this concept is taking itself into being received by the masses crowd and making its presence much more meaningful & useful. of course. Let's have a word with experts and later we will move further.

Expert Views

Life and death are two indiscernible vitalities of life. Time, also termed as "god's clock", essentially chronicles the proceedings between life and death: from past to present to future. It is significant for every human to understand that our existence in this universe is governed by this "time" factor while, interestingly, we never know the quantum of time allotted to each one of us.

With this milieu, we have two options with us. Either do nothing and allow time to pass (which any way would pass) or do everything possible within the available time. Given a choice, the first option being easier may suit many, but for our social sustenance we get to do our bit, however big or small, it is as per capabilities and skills developed/acquired by each one of us. Nonetheless, the unfortunate part of our life is that we generally do not have life term plans for us, though we may be experts in short term ones. Subsequently, there comes a phase in our life when we realize "inadequate utilization of time".

This sets the context of **"time utilization"** in our life rather than looking at time as a factor to be **"managed".** And exactly, that is what is being enlightened in this book *"There is no time management"*.

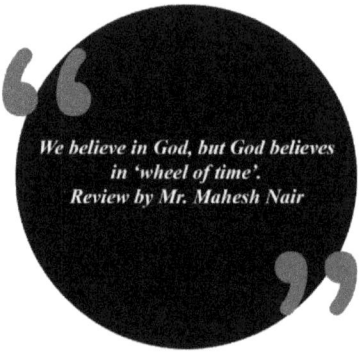

We believe in God, but God believes in 'wheel of time'.
Review by Mr. Mahesh Nair

Sridhar has brought in this wonderful concept of Time Utilization vs Time Management. This concept if understood properly, has a far-reaching significance which is deeply connected with the life of each one of us. Understanding this concept can not only make our lives more meaningful and worthier but also lessen the pain of our past karma which we have accumulated during our past lives.

- Time Management as a concept has its significance in fulfilling our worldly priorities albeit with some struggle.

- Time Utilization seems to have a more holistic & spiritual connotation. It also connotes making the best of whatever time is available to us to achieve the purpose of our life.

Time is a phenomenon experienced only during our earthly sojourn when our ego mind makes us believe that "I am a separate entity". The single most important truth of life is that we are spiritual beings having an earthly experience. Our spirit or Atman is eternity. It is not bound by time.

Desa-kala-vastu-parichheda is the term used to signify the conditioning of our knowledge in terms of space, time, and objects. We cannot think of anything else other than only space, time, and objects. Our entire world of perception only relates to name, form, and action. Names and forms cannot be there unless there is space and time. However, in Pure Existence (One Universal Consciousness), space and time cannot be there.

The ultimate goal of every life and life after life is to discover our true selves.

So, the time we experience during our earthly sojourn is best utilized in re-discovering our true self. This means our every effort (Physical, Mental, Emotional, and Intellectual) goes only towards achieving this goal.

The sooner we realize this, the sooner we will be able to rid ourselves of our pain. In our current life, we all have come with a bank balance of past life Karmas (Prarabdha). The path towards discovering our true self implies two things: (1) lighten our load of past karma and (2) do good new karma (without the ego consciousness that you the DOER).

Every moment of your precious time must, therefore, be utilized in performing actions that nourish your spirit and invoke well-being on every level. Contribute to the wellness of yourself, your family, your organization you serve, your society, your nation, and the world at large. Every moment of your life should be used in asking "How can I serve" rather than asking "What's in it for me."

Every moment of your life utilized in this manner would not only liberate you from past karma but also enable you to experience the miracle of liberation to fulfil the greater purpose of your life.

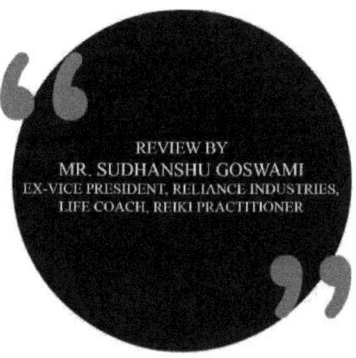

REVIEW BY
MR. SUDHANSHU GOSWAMI
EX-VICE PRESIDENT, RELIANCE INDUSTRIES,
LIFE COACH, REIKI PRACTITIONER

Time Grid Matrix

Time management vs time utilization provided insights of the TIME - ever diminishing resource for an individual. My sight got stuck at time grid matrix, which is a very effective way to improve efficiency and effectiveness, as both are linked to time and quality. In my opinion, the matrix is a closed loop practice, in electronics we call as PLL. Actions related to different roles played by an individual can be embedded into this matrix. Effectiveness depends on, one's action to the findings of the post-mortem at the end of the day and end of the week of this matrix, i.e., how much % time got spent in each quadrant and which quadrant gives efficiency and effectiveness leading to the best possible way of time utilization. The entire game is about keeping on correcting the plan based on the findings and arriving at the optimum plan. The critic may say, it is a time taking activity, but actually it is sharpening the saw.

REVIEW BY
MR. Y SOMAYAJULU
EX CTO RELIANCE JIO
PRESENTLY - STUDENT

My thoughts

The booklet on There is No Time Management is a novel one. The initiative by Sridhar Yerramilli to bring out the concept of time utilization is a novel one. We only learnt about time management all these years and actively propagated the concept. This concept of time utilization is an eye opener.

The introduction given in the form of his beloved daughter's thoughts who left for heavenly abode is mind boggling. This brilliant child has taught us the meaning of life and effective utilization of available time. I appreciate the effort and hope the readers will assimilate the concepts and utilize for their own benefit. My best wishes to all the readers and Shri Sridhar for introducing this novel concept.

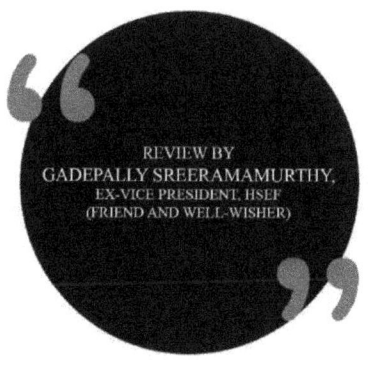

REVIEW BY
GADEPALLY SREERAMAMURTHY,
EX-VICE PRESIDENT, HSEF
(FRIEND AND WELL-WISHER)

Sridhar Yerramilli

"Expertise in Time Utilization"

Let's move on to the next chapter, "Prepare yourself to get Expertise in Time Utilization".

Please note that the term Time Management will be used in this publication an umpteen number of times, but only in the context of the current practices existing throughout the world. Of course, the old term will be strikethrough to Pop up a message that... There is no..., you know it better now and hence I have not taken the pain to repeat it.

The Time Management sessions which I have attended, almost 20 to 30 sessions, the core focus area was time management in terms of Office time. How to manage Office time to improve organizational productivity.

Right. If that would not have been the agenda of Organizations, why would they spend lots of time and finances to build the competency of their employees. Again, I am right. Hope we are on the same page.

But dear Readers, if you don't have the discipline in your complete lifestyle, you are still the same. Even if you get the training 1000 times each year, you can't instill this discipline partially, only for the office timings. This link was missing in many trainings I attended and hope the same with you, and this alone is the reason organizations need sessions every now and then to keep their employees reminded about… again the term Time Management.

What exactly I wish to say is, any habit is a habit for the total package of life and cannot be partially adopted. If you have time management as a habit, it would be for your entire life and not partially for the office hours or for personal hours.

Take an example of myself only, as a chain smoker in teenage years, I was working in my workshop and every now and then I had to turn off the machinery and go for a smoke. Similarly, after closing down the workshop I also used to smoke in the same fashion. By god's grace and my will power I discarded the pollutant factor from my life, but the point I am trying to make out is, I used to smoke round the clock and not only at office or personal times.

Similarly, after each so-called Time Management training, I was back to normal. After due thought process and brainstorming I got the culprit and that was the little word Time Management and when I have started changing my perception from the term Time Management to Time Utilization, I was back on time.

So, the conclusion for the above is, this book focusses on overall time Utilization and not partial time management. You will envisage and experience a drastic change in your life from the time from when you have changed your perception from Time Management to Time Utilization, till the time almighty has given you the quota to breathe (Oxygen, the most perishing resource which we are trying to revive).

[Do a plantation of your choice, at least one per month and encourage your family members too. See the change calculation below.

My Current Age = 44, My Life expectancy = 85 years, Plantations per year = 12, total Plantations = 12 X 41 = 492, the total for a family of 4. Total family plantations per year = approx.-2000 in my lifetime. Wow! Someone has to come and pat my back; it is splendid work! Isn't it?]

You may be thinking; this guy is again going out of context... Hold On. The above message is only a bookmark. I am taking a break and will start to write again in a while. So, you too can take a break here and get back again.

"Role Identification"

I think I was a good catalyst for the chemical reaction in between, my Concept and your Brain and the outcome is turning Green, (Positive).

Now let's move on to Role Identification. But before that, I need to address a question of my critic, again the same fellow who inspires me to have critical jargon for the concepts.

Critic: - Is our life a job? What roles are you taking about? Silly

Me: - Wait a Minute bro.., read the concept below and then you will get the answer.

Role Identification:

Many of us think of roles when we join an organization. We apply for those roles by reading the job description of such roles. Am I right? Yes! Obviously. Many of whose eyes are currently plotting these words including myself once applied for a job either as a Junior Engineer, Executive, and Supervisor etc. and moving up the career ladder. Some are moving faster grabbing the opportunities and some are struggling to make up their pace. Whatsoever, we are being introduced to the role culture after formal education and landing up on a Job.

But let us understand that a role is also immediately born along with us. It unfolds itself as we grow, in each and every direction our mind focusses. Sometimes, these roles are also automatically created without us even knowing them. As human beings, we have to have space & time allotted for every role we are in, either knowingly or unknowingly.

When we can't cope with this, the resultant is the five-letter word STRESS with an additional bonus of a basket full of health issues.

For instance, let us look into a hierarchy of roles of a girl child for a full lifecycle. This will give you a clear understanding of my intention. As soon as the girl child is born, she is a daughter to her parents, now here role is only that of a daughter. Gradually she grows up, she will become a student, it may so happen that a baby boy is born to the parents and this daughter is now a sister also.

Moving forward, she will build up friends & foes, new relationships, once graduated if she joins any employer, now the role of employee adds up. Later she marries & now she takes up the role of wife, a daughter-in-law, sister-in-law etc. ones she again gives birth to a baby boy or girl, she becomes a mother. Likewise, if you observe, life starts with one role and gradually roles are accumulated added, Daughter, sister, granddaughter… Mother etc.

In an indirect sense, or why to call it indirect, let me be direct, as our roles add up, our responsibilities grow, and our time is divided in whichever proportion it may be. Am I right? Yes again.

Again, let's take an example, when we start our schooling, we have only rhymes and games in playschool and nursery, gradually different subjects are introduced and the school time is equally divided into periods, mostly 45 Mins per slot, later on when we reach a particular level, say graduation or even higher, the toughness of the subject increases and number of subjects decrease, time is again slotted equally.

Once we are out of academics after graduation or any level of education, we reach an office. Now 8 hours in the office and 16 hours outside, a general equation. But here, at this point of time, if we are observant, we have all other roles with an additional role of an employee. But the role of full-time student is replaced with employee.

Gradually, as we engage ourselves self in this new role and move on, unknowingly, we start killing most of the roles and focus on our career. Slowly the 8 hours' time becomes 10, workload increases, these imbalances the life and then starts affecting our productivity.

Sometimes we even feel that we had interests & hobbies, likes, which we have almost forgotten. When someone sings a song which you sang once upon a time, your mind says "I wanted to sing" but there was no time and now it's almost impossible. Singing is just an example, there are millions of hobbies, friends, interests even relations being killed with the so-called limitation of time.

Unfortunately, it becomes too late when we realize this, and our soul turns unhappy, while we try to search for answers.

Friends I am truly clear that we become unhappy eventually as we are unable to justify the roles. I am not saying that this is the case with all, but each one of us is surely suffering with such a case. This is because either we are ignorant of the roles we have to fulfil or demean their existence duly prioritizing only limited roles.

This is the reason; I have come up with role identification. We have to identify the roles which we have to fulfil. Some roles are inevitable, some are needed of the hour, some roles are instantaneous, some are pleasure giving, some are wish-fulfilling. Whatever may be the reason, we should have a clear understanding of the roles.

Let's take my case as an example for Role Identification. I am listing down my roles, which in any case I wish to justify, not for the world but for myself.

I have to serve the Roles of a Son, a brother, husband, father, social worker, musician, a Chef, a Sports person, a spiritual seeker, an Employee, a student, a Guide/Coach/Mentor/Speaker, Author, lethargic person, an entrepreneur, friend.

And the list go on and on, may increase or decrease with time and focus…

So, in short, now I have my roles, OMG 15 + numbers, but these many roles, isn't it hard to imagine I have so many roles. May be, but these many roles exist in my life, that's undoubted truth.

Now that I am clear about my roles, how to proceed further.

Hang-on, I am clear about my roles, but are you? Please list down the roles you are performing and also do include any roles which you wanted to be a part of, a hobby, passion etc. Doesn't matter whether this role is live or not. Together we will make up a way.

The simple truth is that unless we know what we are and what we have to do, we can't do that. So, once we are clear about what we want to achieve we can think about the HOW aspect.

Remember: There are certain roles which motivate us to perform other roles. Did not get me. Relax, I will ensure you understand this. A software guy who is really stressed with loads of work to perform, may wish to resign the job every second, but he continues, because he has to pay his monthly EMI for a costly house, Car, pay school fee of his child, pay the grocery bills etc. Even wishing to leave a role, you saw how other roles became motivational blocks (blocks in this case are steps to move ahead and not hurdles) for him to continue his role as an employee.

You can call these later roles motivational roles which always let us take positive steps, not letting us take quick disappointing decisions. How many of the current readers are still continuing with roles they wish to leave, due to such motivational roles. ☺ I am one of them of course.

Now that we are clear with the role identification part, before moving ahead towards planning, take a deep breath and say to your mind, "Whatever I wish to achieve, I have to put my Time & Effort". I have to apply the P2P formula.

Now, I wish to bring in a formula at an introductory level so as to ensure we are not moving out of the context and at the same time knowing this concept now will elevate our thought process.

The **D Cube Formula (D^3).** My critic pointed out. "Hey Sridhar, are we now moving to mathematics?" you say P2P, D^3.

Yes, of course! Life is full of Mathematics, isn't it? A limited amount of time which is different for every individual but reducing equally for all.

Let's come back to the formula.

D^3 is nothing but **D**esire→**D**ream→**D**eserve.

We all will have desires, we dream too, but often the missing link is**, we forget to get deserving**. We don't become a deserving soul for the desire and often our desires become only daydreams.

Never miss the link anymore:

The crucial point to stress here is, we have dreams, desires and they become daydreams only because we don't put our focus, energy, and effort to become deserving to fulfil our dreams, desires.

For instance, a person wishes to become a body builder, but every day he lifts only 3 KG dumbbell for every piece of exercise, say triceps biceps etc. He will become fit but not a body builder. Guess why? Because, unless you change your weights at a regular frequency and have stress on the muscles, they will never grow. In order to fulfil a dream or desire, we have to work on it, stretch a bit out of the comfort zone and then only we will achieve it, because we have to become deserving.

What I want to convey is, you have identified the roles which you have to perform, then stretch a little bit to habituate the same and achieve the happiness derived out of the role.

Roles & happiness? Yes, Of Course, when you were the first-time father and that too, a father of a girl child, were you not happy. All those who have not yet taken up the role, learn from others' experience and comment to yourself.

Here after D Cube (Dreams, Desires & Deserving) we bring the next formula P2P.

P2P is nothing but **Plan** to **perform:** - Have a concrete plan for whatever you wish to perform.

So now let's move on to PLANNING, the most important aspect of **Successive Success or Failure...** and yet the least used and most ignored tool.

There Is No Time Management

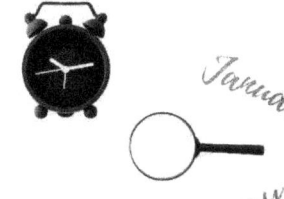

Planning

Planning is an integral part of each and every activity wherein we put our effort to obtain any desired output. Is this true? Please answer this question sincerely.

Well, I feel we plan for some activities in life, this is true for only some of the cases, where we don't own the control of the activity.

What does this mean? This means planning is done only for partial tasks of our life. Some tasks are controlled by circumstances and others are done by us. But what is the magnitude of the tasks which we plan? Say for example, we have to board a flight and flight departure is not in our control. So, we plan to go to the airport on time. For instance, we had control on flight departure, let me tell you even a single flight may not have proceeded to destination. Funny, isn't it, but true?

Chance (or) Choice:

Almost in every conversation with any stranger I encounter for the first time, I have a question,

Are you, in this position, what you are now, BY CHOICE or BY CHANCE?

The answer I receive most of the time is, by Chance.

After Primary, Secondary, Senior Secondary Education, when students have to take admission into graduation, in the last-minute the thinking starts, medical stream or engineering stream? Shall I opt commerce? Is CA a better option?

Now the decision lies at the mercy of the parents, the percentage they obtained in the entrance examinations and many more certain barriers/hurdles. This is one step. Later, after completion of the graduation, campus interviews, jobs, again a set of hurdles.

We often see many engineers of other streams becoming software engineers. Graduates land a job not even closer to their streams or in fields where they have not even imagined themselves to be, or they were even not aware of the field.

That's the reason for the question, put here once again. Are you, in this position, what you are now, BY **CHOICE** or **BY CHANCE?**

Nowadays, graduation and post-graduation have become the benchmark for jobs, but again to what jobs, whichever comes into the way and not of the choice of the seeker.

We plan for a party, a movie, a travel, even to go beyond, we plan for projects in organization, but why is it so, we are reluctant, ignorant or any other word of your choice to plan for the **biggest project in life, which is life itself.** Why are we flowing along with the water, why not swim against the odds and let our dreams come true? It's not that no one is doing so, those who are planning their life are becoming legends, those thousands of names in the total population of whichever country you belong to, which we remember, or turn up into quiz questions.

Who is the culprit for this set of words in the above paragraph, I feel, we as parents, teachers, guides, mentors are failing to create the sense of this planning in our children, because mostly we never did it? We left our life to be a Chance and let the same legacy thoughts continue for decades like the one "Time Management", which never existed. These words may be harsh, but surely true.

Planning should start early in our life, if it was not in the case of **y(our)** lives, let it be the case in the lives of our children, so that next generations improve.

Does it make sense to think in this direction? For me yes, it is, and for you, your decision.

Ok, the answer for the earlier question "Are you, in this position, what you are now, BY CHOICE or BY CHANCE? May be by **Chance**, but what should be the answer for next question below,

"From now onwards, can we make our life a **choice** and not merely **a chance**" what do you say friends.

If your Answer is still No, you may cease reading beyond this line and if the answer is a big yes, then plan, plan and plan every second from now.

You have two options.

Heat up the iron rod for 5 minutes and hit 10 times with a sledgehammer to bring it to your desired shape.

(Or)

Heat up the iron rod for 15 minutes and hit once or twice with a sledgehammer to bring it to your desired shape.

Planning is like heating up the rod to such an extent that only one or two hits will change its shape.

I loved a quote by **Alan Lakein** which I read on google last night.

"Planning is bringing the future into the present so that you can do something about it now."

80% of planning and 20% of execution is all needed to get the desired results. (80/20 Pareto Law)

Now we have spent a considerable amount of time to understand planning. But in this context, the context of time utilization, what to plan? How to plan?

Yes, I got your question. In the earlier chapter, we had role identification. Hope you remember the roles identified by you.

Now we have to segregate the roles in different buckets, **Must Have, Good to Have, Not to Have etc.**

This is nothing but to prioritize the roles which we have decided to perform.

Ok, let me pull in my roles and do this exercise for you.

My Roles, the Role of a Son, a brother, husband, father, social worker, musician, a Chef, a Sports person, a spiritual seeker, an Employee, a student, a Guide/Coach/Mentor/Speaker, Author, lethargic person, an entrepreneur, friend is to be segregated into different buckets.

Must Have: Roles of a Son, a brother, husband, father, Employee,

Good to Have: A Chef, a Sports person, a spiritual seeker, a Student, a Guide/Coach/Mentor/Speaker, Author, lethargic person, an entrepreneur, friend.

Motivational: musician, Social Worker, a Coach/mentor/Speaker/Author.

Not to Have None:

In short, I have three categories, *must have*, those roles which I am bound to perform and *good to have,* those roles which I wished to perform but without these roles, life will keep going but with a sort of unhappiness or a vacuum, because I really love these roles and would be happy to see that they are a part and parcel of my life span. The third category are the **Motivational Roles** as well which keeps my spirits up.

Now once we have categorized the roles, "FREEZE, FREEZE & FREEZE".

Don't let any weakness stop you from performing the roles. The only strength is the affirmation which we have made, the will is the strongest weapon which can win many odds of the war and ultimately the war itself.

As you have observed, I have categorized some roles in the motivational category. These roles inspire me to do almost anything. Sometimes when I feel like stuck up in some must have roles and not being able to cope up/stressed up, I immediately switch to these roles which strengthens me to get back to my work.

Say my work is feeling like routine, I pick up a role from the motivational category and raise my spirits and get back to work.

This is what I call **MOTI-TASK** (Sridhar's MOTI TASK).

Likewise, you too add some roles in the motivational category to have your **MOTI-TASKS**.

Now the next task is to chalk out the time to be provided for each role. This is where you create a space for everything.

TIME for Everything & Everything in its TIME. Let this be the motto for this time lining task.

I have shown below time slotting for each of my roles as an example.

Roles	Performance Time	Remarks
Son, Brother, Husband, Father	24X7X365(X lifetime)	
Employee	8:45 to 18:00 hrs. X 6 Days	Only in Office Timings
Chef	09:00 am to 03:00 PM Only on Sundays	I Cook for my family every Sunday
A Spiritual Seeker	30 Mins Monday to Friday	
A lethargic Person	Every Saturday	I just pass my Time on Saturdays
A Sports person	Play Cricket, shuttle/Chess/	

	Ludo/Business etc. for 1-2 hours per Week, 5 KM of cycling every day from Sunday till Friday	
A Musician	2 Hrs. of Music Practice Everyday	
A Student	30-60 Mins everyday	Learn something new each day
A Guide/Coach/ Mentor/ Speaker, Author, Friend	30-60 Mins as and when needed reserved for these activities	
An entrepreneur	30-60 Mins	Capture some new business ideas & build project plans

If you observe in the above table, for some roles even though we can't have specific timings and the role extends dawn to dusk, the actual amount of time needed to spend is very little. Say for example, if you are living away from your family or Mother due to certain dependencies, make a habit of spending 10 mins talking to them over the phone rather than being busy all day and just sending a message. This will ensure a healthy relationship and justify your role as a son/Parent/Husband etc.

Similarly, I am good at culinary arts, but I can't spare the entire week in the kitchen. So, I have taken the opportunity every Sunday to cook for my family and give them some relaxation for at least half of the Sunday. **My motivation for doing so is Mr. Ravichandran Nageswaran, my earlier Manager and a good friend of mine. I visited his home and found him cooking while his family were enjoying the moment. It is not about the taste of the food but is about the taste of joy in spending time.**

As Employees/Students, we have at least a Sunday or even Saturday & Sundays Off but do our mother/Wife those who cook for us have any holidays. So sometimes at least try and give them an off. If you can't cook, schedule a lunch/dinner at any restaurant of their choice twice monthly. Isn't it a promising idea? Generally, we do this occasionally.

Tip: Start learning to cook and let me tell you, this will turn into the most fascinating job of yours. Cooking teaches you many things in life, such as how much salt you have to use, what portion of spices are good to make the dish tasty. You can correlate the same with life on how much we have to engage with which relationship. Even though we use less salt when compared to the quantity of the overall dish, it makes the dish tastier. Use the salt less or more than required, gone is your dish right.

Also, I have taken up the role of a lethargic person every Saturday. I just relax during the day both at home and at the office. I am not serious in any activity on Saturdays and feel this as my right.

Finally, I have done the above exercise for you. I have **time for everything**, and I ensure that I **do everything on Time.**

Life is too small to waste time and in the initial 15 to 20 years our time is wasted with unlimited excuses like, "Ok, we will do", "there is still time", "ok he is still too small to understand" etc. and lack of maturity.

Please understand that, as now we all are grown up and let us improve ourselves. Also, we should now be able to explain these significant things to the children from their initial stages and make sure the message that, "these little things make a huge difference" go well into their little minds. This is how we can change the forth coming generations; we are already $¼$, $½$, and $¾$th done with our lives.

This last sentence is not applicable to children and teenagers reading this book.

Remember: I do not feel that watching TV, a movie, playing a game as time pass or wasting time. They are part of my life but again, **everything in its time**.

Example: Do we sit in an examination hall thinking of a movie or a sport? Sure, we will not, that is the time for answering the question paper. A limited number of people may say we do think of a movie or planning a game. Yes, it is true for those who are not prepared for the exam and wish to pass time.

When you have **time for everything** and **everything is done on time**, you never feel that life is monotonous, nor do you feel you are spending too much time in any activity, office/studying etc.

Now, I am not going to tell you that this much time is right for this activity or have this many numbers of hours to study. You are mature enough to judge. Are you not? I feel yes.

However, in the later chapter while we discuss ethical time utilization, we will cover a bit of it, but again time slotting decision will be all yours.

Practice the Roles & Time Slots

Now that we have our roles and time slots for the roles, it is the time to practice these roles according to the time slots created. It is always important to have a **"To Do List"** for everyday tasks and have a glance of the same when we wake up having a cup of coffee/Tea to whatever you are habituated.

A small tip, have your place set for the coffee/tea with a table and the "to do list" or a white board available there readily so that you do not forget. But again, please do not have this "to-do list" in your mobile as this little gadget is a great time stealer and will distract you without your knowledge.

Remember practice makes man perfect, the same is applicable for women too. 😊

Here again, I am with another important formula, the formula is A^3 (A Cube). These small formulae being written in the book are easy to remember. I will also summarize the formulae in the end where in you can refresh them once again.

Now coming back to **"A Cube,"** please try to understand this formula as this will prove to be very important for your future.

A Cube = **A**ccept, **A**djust & **A**void.

Accept: Accept the roles you have planned to perform, accept the time slots

Adjust: Adjust your mind to the change. Adjust yourself for the roles. Adjust your routine and timelines.

Avoid: Avoid internal conflict, avoid dilemmas, and avoid anything & everything which you feel will hinder your acceptance and adjustment.

Here is an especially important tip for you. You should have someone who believes in you, your thought process, supports you, motivates you as a guide, a philosopher with whom you can share these thoughts and get motivated.

Another important thing is that you are the best someone for yourself other than any outsider who can Inspire & I know you got it.

I have another Idea for you to adjust, but prior to that understand that you will be able to adjust to anything which you accept. So, keep on accepting & embracing the positives and also keep an eye on the weaknesses, negative factors as well.

Let us be very precise, we will have both positives and negatives in life without which life will not exist. If you have some negatives, it is ok, and then only you will have the possibility to act on them and make it positive. Even a battery without a negative terminal will not work and how come a life will work without a negative.

Understand that you and only you can get to know your **SWOTs** and only you can change them to the desired quadrant.

SWOT May be a new term for some of the friends. Let me explain, **SWOT** is an acronym for **Strengths, Weakness, Opportunities, Threats.**

This is segregated into 4 quadrants as shown below,

Strengths	Weakness
1.	1.
2.	2.
3....	3....
Opportunities	**Threats**
1.	1.
2.	2.
3....	3....

Now list out the roles in the four quadrants, which role is a strength for you, which is your weakness, where do you find opportunities to improve & where do you see threats.

Now, we have to focus on the weakness to convert into strengths, similarly threats to be converted to opportunities or strengths.

This seems to be rocket science, doesn't it? Absolutely not. Just try it out and you will see it unfolds and clears the path for the next level.

Let me explain how I overcame my weakness. My weakness was to keep an eye on the time slots for every day. I found it difficult to keep track of my time and activity. So, I started to use google calendar and now google calendar reminds me of the routine.

Caution: You should use such technology only if you have practiced using the same for the purpose you start using it. Else as told earlier these little gadgets are great.

You got it right.

If there is a will there will be a way. Agreed? Hope yes. So, keep your spirit high and complement it with your willpower, you can achieve anything you desire and deserve.

Let us focus about getting habituated with the roles and practicing them religiously every moment.

Now you have to analyze your daily routine. One must be profoundly serious to perform this analysis as this would be the current level or benchmark to measure your success.

Tip: Success is not a past tense, present tense, or future tense. Success is present continuous tense, and it is always hand in hand with failure. Please understand, if there is no failure, there is no need to succeed.

Pen down every activity from the time you wake up till your sleep. Just invest in a small pocketbook and start writing the time spent for each and every activity. Seriously I did this.

This activity has two advantages. The first advantage is we can assess how many roles are being performed every day knowingly or unknowingly. Secondly, we will get to know the magnitude of tasks being performed which will be helpful to convert the time utilization for something more useful. This will be elaborated in the next chapter.

So, once you have the list of tasks, segregate them with respect to the roles. And guess what? Amazing! You will find that most of the time slots are covered in this activity.

This will definitely inspire you to improve yourself at a much faster pace than expected. Also identify which roles need attention, which roles are to be avoided etc.

Seriously, this is not a challenging task. Many of us may feel this is a silly way, but believe me, this is the only way to improve ourselves. Without having known, where we are, is it right to plan where to go? Yes, it is, but friends, it is not right on planning how to go. Presume you all agree to my thoughts.

So, now after this exercise, you know which roles are being performed, which roles are to be performed, which are to be avoided. Now select a role which you are overdoing, practice to regulate it to the time slot you have mentioned in planning.

Example: If you find yourself most of the day busy being busy without productivity or busy being lazy the entire day try to regulate it.

Do not hurry up, only one role which is to be regulated. Similarly, select a role which has to be adjusted as per the time slot and try adding more time to it.

Also select one role which is to be avoided and try to avoid it.

After you have achieved one set of all the tasks, practice them for 2 weeks. Then perform the activity to list down the entire day's tasks. If you find improvement, continue to follow the same plan. If not, again to "A Cube."

Some might find that, in the first instance of your practice, you will achieve the desired results, some might need a little extra time and effort to get habituated. I will not tell you to practice this twenty-one days, forty days etc. these are merely numbers for me, and I believe, each individual has their own timelines to get habituated or to achieve a desired outcome. Again, I am not falsifying the theory put forward by other intellectuals. As a small example, the average blood pressure of any person is to be 120/80, right? But can you find the same to be true for every individual? It differs by some numbers, mine is always 110/72. I am fit & fine.

So, create your own timelines for your improvement, evaluate it and stick to it. What is important is the **"WILL POWER"** on a particular desire.

A quite common example, when you wish to purchase a car of any brand, you will see only those cars around you. Am I right? I experienced this in many different cases. When you think about someone, suddenly they will call you for no reason. This is the power of will and that of the subconscious mind.

So now we have understood the planning part. Knowingly or unknowingly we all are performing to fulfil our roles and I remember, earlier I said, when you will try to note down the daily activities you get much more clarity on your schedule, you can adjust, avoid, or accept and subsequently you will be able to be a positive outlier in every role you perform.

***Tip*:** Perfectness: Do not search for perfectness in everything, as the definition for your perfectness may change with that of others or even your perfectness differs for one task to other.

Example: If you wish to become a perfect cook, believe me you can never be that one.

There Is No Time Management

Identify Your Time Stealers

Time stealers? I heard about people stealing our wealth, money etc. but who are these time stealers? It is especially important to know about time stealers. Wealth, if stolen may be accumulated again over a period of time, but time stolen can never be reversed. The first and foremost-time stealers in our lives is ourselves only. Yes, you heard it right. "Let us do it after an hour," "let us do it tomorrow," "Oh there is still more time" right these are some of the sentences we often use. Isn't it? These sentences and the root cause of these sentences, which is our attitude towards the activities and our plans, that they can be suspended or postponed as we still have lots of time is the biggest time stealer. And there is good news that we can arrest this stealer ourselves with a little practice. Let me tell you that I am not a big hero in doing so, I am also still practicing it. If I were a hero in arresting this time stealer, this book should have been completed 3 months earlier

😊. So, we all are facing the same problem and let us try to arrest this stealer ASAP.

The second set of time stealers is technology or social media. WhatsApp, Facebook, Twitter, Tic Tok, Mojo, sharechat and the list goes on. Did you ever imagine how much time we spend on these? There is no harm in spending time on social media but there should be a check. If we open Tic Tok, we just scroll down and down and suddenly we realize it is already an hour since we have scrolled down. Right? Same is the case with other social media platforms. I am not asking you to stop spending time on social media, instead asking you to limit the time with your consciousness. I realized this and started restricting. But how? I used to keep my mobile away from myself. When it rang, I used to go and answer the call. I made a habit to reply to WhatsApp only once every 2 hours for 10 mins. Likewise, I restricted Facebook only for 2 days in a week. So, you can have your own plan to restrict the usage.

The next set of time stealers are phone calls, people dropping in without notice. Unproductive meetings, unplanned actions and you can list many more.

A particularly valuable tool for organizing our time according to the priority of the activities is the time grid matrix. This is a table-like structure given below which could be used to prioritize our activities and execute them in the same priority.

2 x 2 Matrix	Urgent	Not Urgent
Important		
Not Important		

Table: Time grid Matrix

If you carefully observe the above 2 X 2 matrix, you can divide all your activities into four quadrants as given below.

1. **Urgent X Important:** activities which are both Urgent & Important.
2. **Not Urgent X important:** activities which are important but not urgent.
3. **Urgent X not important:** Activities which are urgent but not so important.
4. **Not Urgent X Not Important:** activities which are not urgent and not important.

So, note down all the activities in these four quadrants which give us an idea on how to prioritize our activities and now you can also decide which tasks are to be addressed first and which tasks can be ignored. Maintain a whiteboard with these four quadrants mentioned on it and note down the tasks in any of the quadrants as and when you come across any task.

The second valuable tool to arrest time stealers is the art of saying NO. Yes, saying no is an art and science as well. In general, we say 'YES' to people we like and say 'NO' to people whom we dislike. We decide yes and no depending on people but not on the job they bring to us. Am I right? But henceforth, try saying yes or no to people and the tasks they bring to you according to your schedule and time grid matrix. As any task reaches you, the first thing you should do is to prioritize the task and write it down in the time grid matrix and then give them a date/time of completion.

One of my critics asked, is it really needed to live a life like this? Avoiding all the social media platforms, leaving all enjoyment, following timelines, where will this lead us to?

My answer is to answer these following questions, for what are we here? What sort of life are we willing to lead? Do we want to achieve anything in our life or just lead the life as it takes us and makes for us? If we do not have a goal in life, if we wish to live a life as time takes us through, no goals, no plans, and then I recommend to you to stop reading this book immediately and get back to your old life.

PS: Remember, may be only 1 % of the total population are known to be the greatest scientists, entrepreneurs, inventors, discoverers, and we are enjoying their efforts. Why can't we reach the stage, what is the difference between us and them? The answer is simple. It is our attitude towards life. Come, let us change our attitude towards life, live like a legend even if it is in our social circle. Let people remember us even when we are away from them. How is this possible? You try to answer this yourself and let us move ahead.

Sridhar Yerramilli

Keeping Ourselves Motivated

The most difficult part which I have identified so far is to have the mind motivated to perform our day-to-day duties with consistency. We plan and follow it for a few days, gradually without our knowledge we derail and lose focus. Sometimes we have breakers such as leaves holidays etc. and we tend to delay intentionally and when we are back to our normalcy in daily life, we find it difficult to get back on our schedule. Is this the case with you as well? Do not worry, this is the case with 100% of the population. But the minds which strive hard to re rail on to the track are the toughest and achieve whatever they want. Fortunately, life gives us many examples. Even when we start to walk for the first time in childhood, we fall, we get up, and we fall again and get up. It is a constant effort which finally makes us walk. But one thing what we forget is, if you try to recollect what parents do, especially mother and grandparents, they constantly motivate the child by clapping, by saying kind words saying 'you can do, try again' etc. This motivation is required even for us. But some feel shy, some ignore, and some feel we are not able to perform and some even think we are hopeless and are not focused.

So, do not worry because we all are in the same boat. The only difference is that high performers constantly search for motivation and keep themselves inspired. It is easier said than done. But how to do it? Let us have a few tools for the same.

Once you prepare your roles, time grid matrix, SWOT Analysis, goal settings share the same with your family members, your friends, and colleagues, so that all are informed about your schedule, and ask them to help you out in reaching your goals and objectives. Once you discuss these plans with them, they may also like the way you approach them, they will help you and may also start doing so.

Self-appraisal is another crucial tool. Often, we look forward for appraisals from others. But in fact, we must appraise ourselves, we should not wait for others to appraise or to receive incentives, gifts from others. It is best practice to have a goal and a self-appraisal package to motivate ourselves. It may be a small gift or appraisal, but we should take it ourselves.

Thirdly, we must maintain a do to list or a goal sheet and go through it on a daily basis or on regular intervals.

Do you have any other tools to add to the list? If yes, please share the same via email id mentioned at the end of the book. I will be glad to include the same in the list, obviously giving you the credits for the same.

There Is No Time Management

Instill the Mechanism for 24X7X365 X (lifetime)

Goal setting is not a part of this book as we already have set a goal to identify our roles and execute the responsibilities of those roles. That is ok, but how to instill these roles for a lifetime? As told earlier, we will fall and for sure we must get up again. That willpower not to get upset but to get up and set ourselves (Dr. Abdul Kalam's words) is very much needed. Secondly, we must set a DRDD, i.e., **D**aily **R**itual at **D**awn and **D**usk. What is this ritual about which we are talking? This is nothing but preparing a small summary sheet of the roles, responsibilities, timelines of not more than one page and read it after waking up each day without fail. Doing this will send all the data into our subconscious mind and then we will breathe in all the details all the time. In childhood, our parents taught us many things, constantly chasing us to brush our teeth, to bath, to have breakfast, to have lunch, go to school, homework etc. But at the later part of life, does they keep chasing us for all these things? These become our daily rituals and we follow them unknowingly. That is what is required for the former also. So, practicing the DRDD will help us achieve our goals.

Setting Daily Rituals at Dawn & Dusk (DRDD): What may be the rituals to set up at Dawn & Dusk? For instance, waking up at 5 AM, spending some time on our body and mind, exercise or Meditation, Daily Prayer, reading a book or journal, practice paying off gratitude to everyone who made our day or five to ten minutes of self-introspection or maintaining a self-introspection dairy. (Refer page no 45/46)

There Is No Time Management

Ethical Time Utilization

Have you ever heard about "Ethical Time utilization"? This is what we have never heard off nor even ever thought off. But this is one of the culprits due to which we may have failed to achieve what we thought to achieve. If you understand this concept and try to start following it, I bet you would be more productive, more satisfying, more of everything you wish to. A better version of what you are today.

We all have heard different proverbs such as **"A Place for Everything and Everything in its place," "Time for everything and everything in its time."** This is where I have derived this concept. Ethical time utilization is nothing but doing the things in the time we have slotted for or opted for. For example, if we calculate the time, we really work at office every day in the eight hours of time, we will be amazed to know that we work only 3 to 4 hours towards fulfilling office goals or that chunk of the work.

Likewise, the work piles up and one fine day we have to work over times to clear the pile. This is the same for any work we do, whether it is study or sports of work. When we plan and learn to use the time for what it is meant for following the ethics, I name it as ethical time utilization. This is planning the time slots for different activities and religiously following the same in that time with no or minimum deviation.

This may sound silly for some readers, easy for some or whatever your perspective is. But, just get to the roots of this process, you can now understand that this is nothing but a self-disciplined approach and then when you try to do this, you will understand how difficult it is, how important it is. We all do waste our time whatever the ratio it may be and when we try to use the time effectively, we can see miracles happening.

When we are working in an organization or for that sake any household activity, just fix the time and stick to it. For instance, in a business day of eight hours, we have been spending four to six hours for home related work. Is it ethical? In my view it is occasionally ok, but not frequently. When we get habituated to such things, we end up utilizing office time for household activities, Personal time for official activities, frequently working late nights, working on Sundays etc.

So, the conclusion is, observe your habits, change your attitude, plan timings, and follow them religiously. The results achieved can be seen by Self-Introspection.

I read the below quotation in a police station yesterday.

"Your Bad attitude is like a flat tyre; you can't go long until you change it."

Self-introspection

The most spoken word and the least done is **"Self-Introspection."** We all are mostly efficient in judging others but never think of judging ourselves. Self-introspection is the most important and efficient tool to bring a 360^0 view of our self, if used properly. Let us stop judging others for at least 10 minutes a day and utilize that time to introspect ourselves.

I remember, in childhood, we used to go for Balvikas classes, conducted by Sri Sathya Sai Seva Samithi all over India for Spiritual upliftment of children from a tender age. There we had a Self-Introspection dairy in a tabular format. An illustration given below for your reference. Every day at night, we had to spend five minutes of our time before sleep to fill in the dairy. This diary need not to be shown to anyone but is to be filled honestly. What a magnificent method for a notable change in our attitude. We used to do this every day without knowing its importance. That habit itself eventually created the habit of Self-Introspection even after a long break.

Illustration of the Self-Introspection Dairy formulated by Sri Sathya Sai Seva Samithi.

S. no	Description	Mon	Tue	Wed	Thu	Fri	Sat	Sun
1	Wakeup Prayer							
2	Exercises							
3	Morning Prayer							
4	Did I lie today?							
5	Did I hurt Someone Knowingly							
6	Did I hurt Someone Unknowingly?							
7	Lunch Prayer							
8	Did I help someone today?							
9	Did I waste My time?							

As shown in the above illustration, we can formulate a table with the daily rituals we wish to perform and follow this pattern to self-introspect. This will surely bring a change in our attitude and help us to improve our altitude.

There Is No Time Management

Summarizing The Formulae

Right from the beginning, I have mentioned some formulae which will help us to take the right decisions at a point where we are stuck. Those are being summarized here for the ease of readers, so that they can reflect upon and move ahead.

- ***D Cube (D^3):** Dream, Desires & Deserving: We have Dreams and Desires and often think less on becoming a deserving soul to turn them into a reality. Hence many of us are not able to turn them into reality and remain as day dreamers. Watch out for your D^3.

- ***Plan to Perform (P2P):** Planning plays an especially key role in achieving a goal. Hence, have your planning in place.

- ***MOTI-TASK** (Sridhar's MOTI TASK): Sometimes we get out of track while performing any task if it exceeds a time limit, hence it is necessary to take regular breaks. We should identify the tasks which rejuvenate our energy in a short span of time say 5 mins to 10 mins.

- *A^3 Cube: A Cube = Accept, Adjust & Avoid: Not all situations are under our control. At such times we must apply the A Cube (A^3) Strategy. Either we have to accept it, adjust, or avoid it.

- **SWOT Analysis**: This tool is an acronym for "Strengths," "Weakness," "Opportunities" & "Threats" and is used to identify these within ourselves.

- **Time Grid Matrix**: This tool is a crucial one in planning time utilization used to segregate the tasks as Urgent-Important, Urgent-Not Important etc.

- ***DRDD:** Daily Ritual to perform on Dawn & Dusk without fail.

Important: All the Formulae which are marked with an Asterisk * symbol as copyrighted to the author of this book. Other formulae have been sourced from various sources like the internet, other books of knowledge or gained over the years of experience.

Sridhar Yerramilli

Final Words

Life is too small to waste our time in moving towards vague directions. Let us build our life which creates and brings value to ourselves and also to the world. If we carefully observe, an exceedingly small percentage of the world's population is serving the rest of the world. Many discoveries, inventions and innovations have made our life comfortable, and all these discoveries, inventions and innovations are not just a thought but working on them relentlessly. Can we name a discovery or an invention which has just happened by a thought only? It is not at all possible. Every Idea, however big or small it may be, whatever difference it brings to our life or to the lives of others require our minute and undivided attention. We may fall many times, but we should have the capability to rise again. As the famous quote of Dr. Abdul Kalam says, when we fall, we should not get upset but we should try to get up and set ourselves should be the moto of our life. What a life is, which is not useful to ourselves and to the world? Lastly, we all have the capacity to deliver a message to the world. Knowingly or unknowingly we all do so. Then why not try to deliver a message which inspires people to become better versions of themselves, which inspires people to do something extraordinary or something ordinary in extraordinary ways.

This handbook is an attempt made to help individuals to have a better understanding on how to plan and succeed in their lives journey without losing its flavor. Lastly, do not use the content of this book to plan and succeed in such a way that it becomes a stress to you. The content should be used as a compass to have a direction to our life's journey understanding that going directionless and coming back to direction what we set is an integral part of life. Without a goal, we will not have direction, without direction we cannot go directionless and cannot even come back. An author pens down his words on to the paper with his interpretation, but a reader may interpret the same using his own intellect which even may be of a higher magnitude, so please feel free to write back your questions and discuss your understanding and provide inputs which may help in bringing out a much better version of this book for future generations.

- "Be the Change you want to see in your life."

- "Be the change you want to see in society."

- "Be the change you want to see in the world."

Self-Reflection
(This page is intentionally left blank for your self-reflection)

Self-Introspection

After reading the book,

- I was able to correlate my life to the content.... **(Yes/No)**

- If I would have thought in this fashion, my life would have been different.... **(Yes/No)**

- What is the best part, which you would like to pass on to your-someone special to bring a change in to their life?

- Is there anything else which is striking your mind which should have been added? (Share it with me, I will ensure to add the same duly giving credits to you)

Claim your Coaching Session

We all need to learn a lot from the universe, environment, plants, animals, fellow human beings. Especially when it comes to humans, we have enormous learning capabilities. Let us learn together, let me learn from you vice versa. I have created an opportunity. Those who purchase this book are may claim the forty-five minutes (45 Minutes) coaching session. Please follow the below instructions to claim your session.

- Proof of purchase or invoice is mandatory for claiming the session. Please seek an invoice for your purchase. If you have purchased this book online, please download the invoice. If you have purchased a copy of the book from offline stores, seek a hardcopy invoice. Please mail the invoice copy to.

- claim_session@sridharyerramilli.co.in
- Once the details are received, we will validate the same and schedule a session.

Note: A single session of 45 mins for a single invoice will be provided. If we have already received the invoice from another source, we would term the same as a duplicate invoice. For duplicate invoices claims, the discretion remains with the author for provisioning the session.

There Is No Time Management

An Important Return Gift to You, Me & World

We all are born and spend time in this world. We owe a lot to the environment and also have a responsibility to pass it on to the further generations with much better conditions. We all receive the utmost important natural elements Oxygen to breathe and water to drink without which we cannot survive. Giving back to nature is impossible but we can try to protect the environment. With this intuition a part of the funds received from each buyer of this book is utilized for planting and safeguarding a tree at a designated location. We will do this by default as soon as the book is sold out. Either online or offline. Please mail the proof of purchase/invoice copy to **plant_a_tree@sridharyerramilli.co.in.** We shall include a tag on your name.

www.ingramcontent.com/pod-product-compliance
Lightning Source LLC
LaVergne TN
LVHW061620070526
838199LV00078B/7361